KU-311-295

THIS BOOK BELONGS TO...

Name:	Age:

Favourite player:

2019/2020

My Predictions...	Actual...

The Canaries' final position:

The Canaries' top scorer:

Premier League winners:

Premier League top scorer:

FA Cup winners:

EFL Cup winners:

Cavan County Library
Withdrawn Stock

Contributors: Dan Brigham & Peter Rogers

A TWOCAN PUBLICATION

©2019. Published by twocan under licence from Norwich City FC.

Every effort has been made to ensure the accuracy of information within this publication but the publishers cannot be held responsible for any errors or omissions. Views expressed are those of the authors and do not necessarily represent those of the publishers or the football club. All rights reserved.

ISBN: 978-1-911502-76-0

PICTURE CREDITS:
Action Images, Jasonpix, Press Association.

£10

3

CAVAN COUNTY LIBRARY	
30018003199300	
Bertrams	02446524
S/16349	J796.334
11334	€7.15

CONTENTS

AT THE TRAINING GROUND

Come three o'clock on a Saturday afternoon, the fans get to see their heroes in action at Carrow Road.

Matchday is the day the Canaries' players, manager and coaching staff are all preparing for, and focusing on, throughout the week. All that preparation takes place at the club's training ground, well away from the watching eyes of the thousands of fans who flock to Carrow Road in hope of witnessing another winning performance.

The hard work begins in the summer months when the players report back for pre-season training. The players are given a fitness programme to follow over the summer break and the first few days back at the training ground tend to involve a number of fitness tests. The results will enable Daniel Farke's coaching and fitness staff to assess each player's condition and level of fitness to ensure they are given the right workload over pre-season, so that they are fully match fit and raring to go for the big kick-off.

A lot of the work done over the pre-season period is designed to help the players reach a level of fitness that they can maintain for the entire campaign and perform at their maximum throughout the season.

When it comes to winning football matches, it is well known that practice, dedication and preparation are all vital ingredients for success. However, in terms of strength and fitness, rest, recovery and diet also play crucial roles in a footballer's welfare. The Norwich players are not only given the best of surfaces to practice on, but also given expert advice and guidance to ensure that they are fully equipped for the Premier League challenges ahead.

Technology also plays its part in helping the Norwich stars perform to their maximum. Prior to taking to the training pitches, players are provided with a GPS tracking system and heart rate analysis monitors ensuring that all they do can be measured, monitored and reviewed.

And if all goes to plan, the team's drive, commitment and meticulous preparation on the training ground during the week, will pay dividends on matchday.

Training for your hair

7

MARIO
VRANCIC

2018/19

GOAL OF THE SEASON

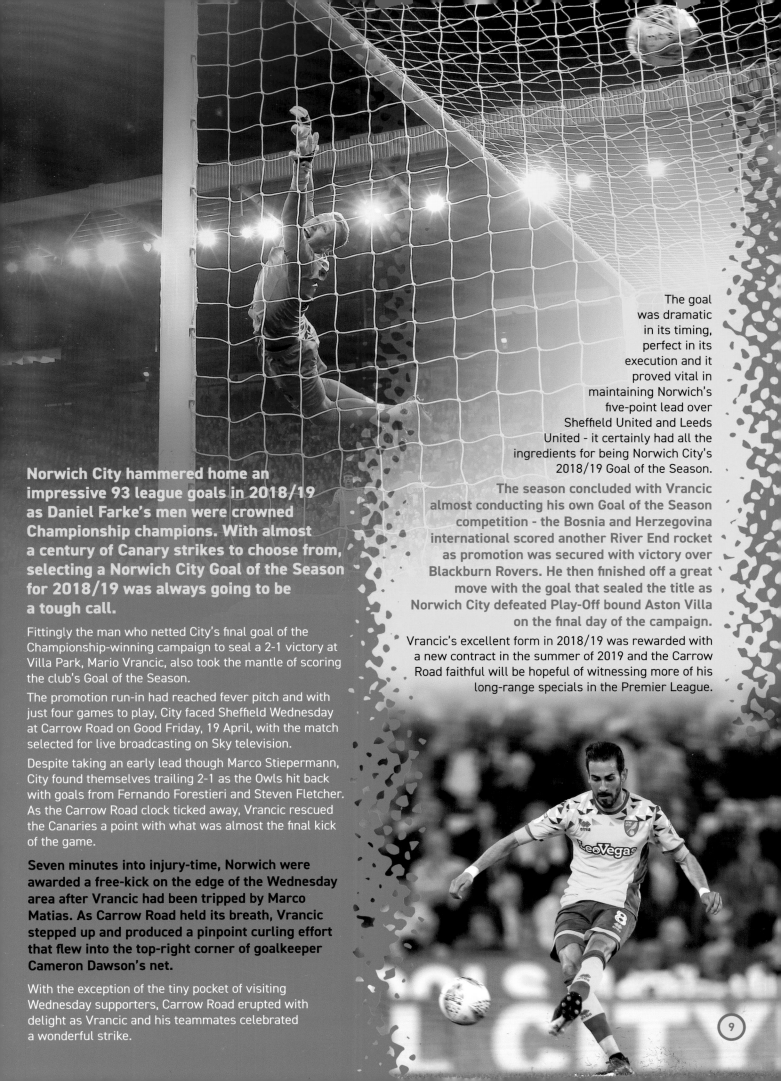

The goal was dramatic in its timing, perfect in its execution and it proved vital in maintaining Norwich's five-point lead over Sheffield United and Leeds United - it certainly had all the ingredients for being Norwich City's 2018/19 Goal of the Season.

The season concluded with Vrancic almost conducting his own Goal of the Season competition - the Bosnia and Herzegovina international scored another River End rocket as promotion was secured with victory over Blackburn Rovers. He then finished off a great move with the goal that sealed the title as Norwich City defeated Play-Off bound Aston Villa on the final day of the campaign.

Vrancic's excellent form in 2018/19 was rewarded with a new contract in the summer of 2019 and the Carrow Road faithful will be hopeful of witnessing more of his long-range specials in the Premier League.

Norwich City hammered home an impressive 93 league goals in 2018/19 as Daniel Farke's men were crowned Championship champions. With almost a century of Canary strikes to choose from, selecting a Norwich City Goal of the Season for 2018/19 was always going to be a tough call.

Fittingly the man who netted City's final goal of the Championship-winning campaign to seal a 2-1 victory at Villa Park, Mario Vrancic, also took the mantle of scoring the club's Goal of the Season.

The promotion run-in had reached fever pitch and with just four games to play, City faced Sheffield Wednesday at Carrow Road on Good Friday, 19 April, with the match selected for live broadcasting on Sky television.

Despite taking an early lead though Marco Stiepermann, City found themselves trailing 2-1 as the Owls hit back with goals from Fernando Forestieri and Steven Fletcher. As the Carrow Road clock ticked away, Vrancic rescued the Canaries a point with what was almost the final kick of the game.

Seven minutes into injury-time, Norwich were awarded a free-kick on the edge of the Wednesday area after Vrancic had been tripped by Marco Matias. As Carrow Road held its breath, Vrancic stepped up and produced a pinpoint curling effort that flew into the top-right corner of goalkeeper Cameron Dawson's net.

With the exception of the tiny pocket of visiting Wednesday supporters, Carrow Road erupted with delight as Vrancic and his teammates celebrated a wonderful strike.

Tim
KRUL

1

POSITION: Goalkeeper **COUNTRY:** Netherlands **DOB:** 3 April 1988

A vastly experienced and popular member of the City squad, Dutch international goalkeeper Tim Krul joined the Canaries from Brighton & Hove Albion in the summer of 2018. He enjoyed a memorable debut season at Carrow Road and was ever-present in the club's Championship title-winning campaign. A great inspiration to the younger players in front of him, Krul pulled off a number of vital saves to help Norwich City ensure promotion to the Premier League.

THE 2019/20 SQUAD

Max
AARONS
2

POSITION: Defender **COUNTRY: England** **DOB: 4 January 2000**

Academy graduate Max Aarons enjoyed an amazing 2018/19 season as he made the Canaries' right-back berth his own and played a major role in the Canaries' promotion to the Premier League. Not only did Aarons end the season with a Championship title-winners' medal, he was also voted the EFL Young Player of the Season at the Football League awards. Rarely beaten in one-on-one situations, Aarons also loves to get forward and support the City attack.

Sam
BYRAM
3

POSITION: Defender **COUNTRY: England** **DOB: 16 September 1993**

A summer signing from Premier League rivals West Ham United, right-back Sam Bryam began his career with Leeds United before stepping up to the top flight with the Hammers in 2016. The 26-year-old's arrival at Carrow Road provides both cover and competition for the right-back berth.

Grant
HANLEY
5

POSITION: Defender   **COUNTRY:** Scotland   **DOB:** 20 November 1991

After injury ruled skipper Grant Hanley out of the majority of the Canaries' 2018/19 success, the captain will be keen to re-establish himself in the City side in 2019/20. Hanley's previous Premier League experience from his time at Blackburn Rovers could prove valuable for City as they come face-to-face with the best teams in the country. A full Scotland international, not only is Hanley a reliable defender, but his height and presence make him a threat at set-piece situations in the opposition's area.

Ben
GODFREY
4

POSITION: Defender   **COUNTRY:** England   **DOB:** 15 January 1998

A powerful and mobile defender, who also has the ability to play in midfield, Ben Godfrey was a real star performer in the Canaries' 2018/19 title triumph. He formed an impressive central-defensive partnership with Christoph Zimmermann in the second half of last season and also chipped in with vital goals away to Rotherham and at home to Reading as Norwich closed in on promotion. His club form was rewarded with a call-up to the England under-20 set-up in March 2019.

Christoph
ZIMMERMANN
6

POSITION: Defender   **COUNTRY:** Germany   **DOB:** 12 January 1993

Giant defender Christoph Zimmermann was voted runner-up in Player of the Season poll following an excellent 2018/19 campaign. After following head coach Daniel Farke from Borussia Dortmund II to Carrow Road in the summer of 2017, Zimmermann produced a number of rock-like performances to make a central-defenders place his own. He skippered the side in the second half of the season in the absence of both Grant Hanley and Timm Klose.

Patrick ROBERTS 7

POSITION: Midfielder   **COUNTRY:** England   **DOB:** 5 February 1997

Capped by England at various youth levels, right-sided midfielder Patrick Roberts became the club's first new addition following promotion when he agreed a season-long loan from Premier League champions Manchester City. Roberts began he career with Fulham, where his early promise saw Manchester City swoop for his services. The 22-year-old has since gained valuable first-team experience with loans spells at Celtic and Spanish side Girona.

Mario VRANCIC 8

POSITION: Midfielder   **COUNTRY:** Bosnia and Herzegovina   **DOB:** 23 May 1989

The goalscoring hero in the final weeks of the Canaries' charge to the Championship title in 2018/19, Mario Vrancic enjoyed an excellent finish to his second season at Carrow Road. Vrancic proved to be a dead-ball specialist and demonstrated that fact perfectly when he expertly equalised with an exquisite last-gasp free-kick against Sheffield Wednesday over the Easter period. He was then on target in both the promotion-winning game at home to Blackburn Rovers and on the final day of the season as City secured the title at Villa Park.

Moritz LEITNER

10

POSITION: Midfielder   **COUNTRY:** Germany   **DOB:** 8 December 1992

Deep-lying midfield playmaker Mortiz Leitner joined the Canaries in the summer of 2018 following a loan spell at the club during the second-half of the previous campaign. Leitner began last season among the substitutes for the opening game of the season, but soon worked his way into Daniel Farke's team. He was on target in the 1-1 East Anglian derby draw at Portman Road, plus the thrilling 4-3 victory over Millwall on 10 November 2019.

THE 2019/20 SQUAD

Onel
HERNANDEZ
11

POSITION: Midfielder **COUNTRY:** Cuba **DOB:** 1 February 1993

Flying-winger Onel Hernandez began an impactful 2018/19 season for the Canaries when he bagged a brace in City's 2-2 opening-day draw with Birmingham City. With electric pace and clever close control, the Cuban-born attacker produced a number of memorable performances in City's promotion -winning campaign. He contributed some vital goals too, most memorably the incredible late equaliser against Nottingham Forest on Boxing Day 2018 as City came from 3-0 down to salvage a point.

Jamal
LEWIS
12

POSITION: Defender **COUNTRY:** Northern Ireland **DOB:** 25 January 1998

Extremely comfortable on the ball and with a burning desire to get forward and support the attack, Jamal Lewis enjoys his forays into the opposition's half, but has the ability to ensure they are not at the expense of his defensive duties. His full-back pairing with fellow Academy graduate Max Aarons was undoubtedly a major factor in the Canaries' promotion success in 2018/19. The defender's club form has already won him full international caps with Northern Ireland despite his tender years.

Todd
CANTWELL

14

POSITION: Midfielder   **COUNTRY:** England   **DOB:** 27 February 1998

Skilful midfielder Todd Cantwell made his mark on the City first team in 2018/19 and scored his first goal for the club in the 3-1 Carrow Road triumph over Rotherham United in December 2018. Another player to progress through the club's Academy set-up, Norfolk-born Cantwell benefited from a useful loan spell with Dutch club Fortuna Sittard in the second-half of 2017/18, before returning to Colney and impressing Daniel Farke.

Timm
KLOSE

15

POSITION: Defender   **COUNTRY:** Switzerland   **DOB:** 9 May 1988

Swiss international defender Timm Klose chipped in with four vital goals in the Canaries' 2018/19 promotion-winning campaign. He netted his first goal of the season heading City in front against Derby County in October 2018 and was on target in the East Midlands again later that month when he scored both goals in a 2-1 win at Nottingham Forest. A positive presence around the squad, Klose scored again to rescue City a vital point from their New Year's Day trip to Brentford.

THE 2019/20 SQUAD

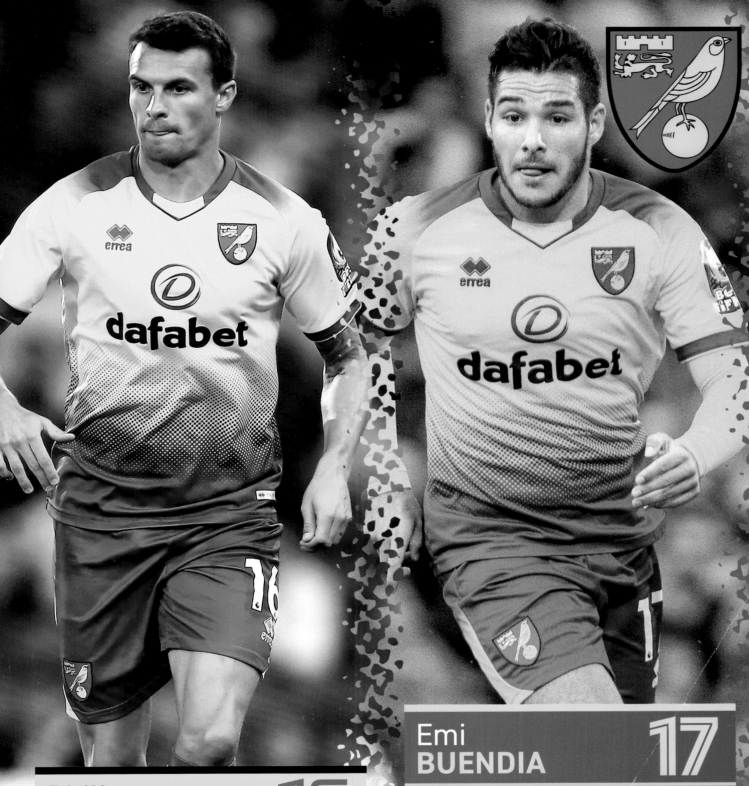

Philip
HEISE
16

POSITION: Defender **COUNTRY:** Germany **DOB:** 20 June 1991

A 2019 January transfer-window signing from Dynamo Dresden, German left-back Philip Heise agreed a three-and-a-half year deal with the Canaries. The 28-year-old defender is comfortable in possession and has great delivery from set piece situations. Heise will certainly be looking to provide some serious competition for the left-back role in his first full season at Carrow Road.

Emi
BUENDIA
17

POSITION: Midfielder **COUNTRY:** Argentina **DOB:** 25 December 1996

The creative spark in the City side, Argentinean playmaker Emi Buendia became a real crowd favourite during his first season at Carrow Road as Norwich City secured the Championship title in 2018/19. With incredible close control, brilliant dribbling ability and a wonderful range of passing skills, Buendia soon established himself as a key member of the City team.

17

Marco STIEPERMANN 18

POSITION: **Midfielder**   COUNTRY: **Germany**   DOB: **3 May 1993**

German midfielder Marco Stiepermann chipped in with nine Championship goals in 2018/19 and ten in all competitions as he enjoyed a highly-productive second season with the Canaries. With good close control and an eye for goal, Stiepermann became one of the first names on Daniel Farke's teamsheet in 2018/19 and agreed a new three-year contract at Carrow Road in May 2019.

Josip DRMIC 20

POSITION: **Striker**   COUNTRY: **Switzerland**   DOB: **8 August 1992**

Norwich City secured the services of Swiss international striker Josip Drmic on a free transfer following their promotion to the Premier League. Drmic was a free agent after being released by Borussia Monchengladbach and his arrival at Carrow Road was seen as a major coup for the Canaries. On target during the tour of Germany and a hat-trick hero in pre-season against Luton Town, Drmic is sure to provide great competition for a striker's role in the 2019/20 Premier League campaign.

Tom TRYBULL 19

POSITION: **Midfielder**   COUNTRY: **Germany**   DOB: **9 March 1993**

Patience was the key for German midfielder Tom Trybull in 2018/19, but in the second-half of the season, he made a place in the City engine room his own. After injury sidelined Alex Tettey, Trybull became recognised as the Canaries' midfield ball-winner and he remained in the side until injury ruled him out of the final two games of the title-winning season. He headed home the third goal in the 3-1 Carrow Road triumph over Birmingham City in January 2019 as Norwich ended a run of five games without a win.

Ralf FAHRMANN 21

POSITION: Goalkeeper   **COUNTRY:** Germany   **DOB:** 27 September 1988

German goalkeeper Ralf Fahrmann joined the Canaries in July 2019 after agreeing a season-long loan from Bundesliga side FC Schalke 04. An experienced stopper, Fahrmann has played approaching 200 games in the Bundesliga and has also competed in European competitions. He will add real quality to the City goalkeeping ranks as the Canaries step up to the challenge of Premier League football.

THE 2019/20 SQUAD

Teemu PUKKI
22

POSITION: Striker   **COUNTRY:** Finland   **DOB:** 29 March 1990

Finland international striker Teemu Pukki fired home an incredible 29 Championship goals in his debut campaign at Carrow Road as Norwich won promotion to the Premier League. Pukki's 29-goal haul saw him etch his name into joint-second place in the list of top Canary league goalscorers in a season. Among his plethora of goals were memorable late strikes in the Carrow Road triumphs over Millwall and Bolton Wanderers, plus an expertly taken brace in the 3-0 East Anglian derby victory over Ipswich Town in February 2019.

THE 2019/20 SQUAD

Ibrahim
AMADOU
24

POSITION: Midfielder **COUNTRY: France** **DOB: 6 April 1993**

Norwich City secured the services of defensive-midfielder Ibrahim Amadou for their 2019/20 Premier League campaign after the former French youth international agreed a season-long loan from Sevilla. Amadou, who also has the ability to operate as a central-defender, became the Canaries' final signing of the 2019 summer transfer window with City also having an option to sign him permanently at the end of the 2019/20 season.

Kenny
McLEAN
23

POSITION: Midfielder **COUNTRY: Scotland** **DOB: 8 January 1992**

An unfortunate injury in the League Cup match with Stevenage in August 2018 prevented Scottish international Kenny McLean from making an immediate impact at Carrow Road following his arrival from Aberdeen. Once back to full fitness, the midfield maestro made a positive contribution across the final weeks of the season - an excellent brace in the 3-2 Carrow Road victory over Bristol City was followed by another goal in the hard-fought 2-1 win victory at Rotherham United.

Alex
TETTEY
27

POSITION: Midfielder **COUNTRY: Norway** **DOB: 4 April 1986**

A regular for the Canaries in their 2014/15 promotion season, Alex Tettey was the only member of the City squad with a Norwich City promotion on his CV when Daniel Farke's men sampled Championship success in 2018/19. The tough-tackling Norwegian midfield international joined the Canaries back in August 2012 and is now the longest-serving member of the first-team squad at Carrow Road.

21

Dennis SRBENY

32

POSITION: Striker **COUNTRY:** Germany **DOB:** 5 May 1994

Due to the form of Teemu Pukki and Jordan Rhodes, striker Dennis Srbeny found first-team opportunities hard to come by during the Canaries' title-winning season. Signed from SC Paderborn in January 2018, Srbeny impressed with two goals in Norwich's League Cup win away to Cardiff City and was also on target as a substitute in the 4-0 win away at Sheffield Wednesday as Norwich went top of the table for the first time during the 2018/19 season.

THE 2019/20 SQUAD

Michael
McGOVERN
33

POSITION: Goalkeeper **COUNTRY:** Northern Ireland **DOB:** 8 July 1984

Northern Ireland international goalkeeper Michael McGovern featured in all five of the Canaries' cup matches in 2018/19, but had to watch from the bench as Tim Krul was ever-present throughout the Championship title-winning campaign. An experienced 'keeper at both domestic and international level, McGovern remains a valued member of the City squad and agreed to extend his stay in Norfolk for a further two years in 2019.

Louis
THOMPSON
34

POSITION: Midfielder **COUNTRY:** Wales **DOB:** 19 December 1994

Clearly a player with great potential and an obvious desire to succeed with Norwich City, Wales under-21 international midfielder Louis Thompson has seen his Canary career interrupted by injury woes. Two serious Achilles heel injuries prevented his progress, but the all-action midfielder certainly has a fan in City head coach Daniel Farke, who handed him a new four-year contract in October 2018.

Adam
IDAH
35

POSITION: Striker **COUNTRY:** Republic of Ireland **DOB:** 11 February 2001

Exciting forward Adam Idah was named City's Academy Player of the Season for 2018/19. The pacy frontman netted 13 goals from 24 appearances for the under-23 side and his form was rewarded with international recognition with the Republic of Ireland at under-21 level. He trained regularly with the first team in pre-season and was handed a Premier League squad number for the 2019/20 campaign.

D  Wears the Birmingham City captain's armband

 Crystal Palace's nickname **E**

Danish Head Coach at Griffin Park **F**

A Chelsea's Spanish skipper

B Do you recognise this Championship club's crest

 The Toffees play their home games here **G**

H  Longest-serving Championship manager and a Millwall legend

 Scored the first home league goal of the season at the City Ground **C**

I Foxes' Nigeria international signing who wears No.8

A Z

2019/20 PART 1

WHO'S WHO &
WHAT'S WHAT
OF ENGLISH
FOOTBALL?

J Manchester City's Brazilian striker who was part of their 2019 Copa América winning side

L This England international has been with the Red Devils since the age of 7

K Polish international midfielder who was ever-present for Leeds United last season

M The Seagulls' Premier League top scorer last season

ONEL HERNANDEZ CELEBRATES
HIS INJURY-TIME EQUALISER AT
BIRMINGHAM CITY TO MAKE IT 2-2

2018/19
will certainly
go down as one
of Norwich City's
greatest campaigns.
Daniel Farke's team
produced an exciting
brand of passing
football and took the
Sky Bet Championship
by storm.

2018/19
SEASON
REVIEW

DELIGHT AT
JORDAN RHODES'
OPENING GOAL V WBA

Certainly not one of the sides fancied for promotion back in the summer of 2018, the Canaries began their campaign away to Birmingham City where a second-half brace from Onel Hernandez proved enough for a share of the spoils.

The first home game of the season was an eventful affair with both Jordan Rhodes and Teemu Pukki marking their Carrow Road debuts with goals. However, a thrilling seven-goal afternoon ended in the favour of visitors West Bromwich Albion who won the match 4-3.

A 2-0 home win over Preston North End in August was sandwiched between defeats away to Sheffield United and at home to early-season pacesetters Leeds United.

City then went into the first East Anglian derby of the season with just four points on the board from a potential 15, as they took to the pitch at Portman Road on September 2, 2018. A 71st-minute equaliser from Moritz Leitner saved the day against Ipswich and preserved City's proud and long unbeaten run against their local rivals. The result also sparked a major upturn in City's fortunes.

Next up was Middlesbrough at Carrow Road where a Pukki goal secured the first of four straight league wins.

With young full-backs Jamal Lewis and Max Arrons joined in the side by fellow Academy graduate Todd Cantwell, the youngsters were playing without fear and their away form was outstanding, typified by an excellent 2-1 win away to Nottingham Forest.

Home wins over Aston Villa and Brentford followed, before City went top of the table for the first time with a 4-0 win away to Sheffield Wednesday. A thrilling 4-3 win at home to Millwall was followed by a third consecutive game of City scoring four - this time in a 4-1 win at Swansea.

The Canaries' never-say-die attitude and ability to score late goals was phenomenal and came to the fore in perfect style when they came from 3-0 down to draw with Nottingham Forest on Boxing Day.

Unbeaten in the league in January 2019, City made a real statement of intent when they returned to the top of the table with an emphatic 3-1 win away to Leeds United on 2 February. After easing past relegation bound Ipswich Town 3-0 at Carrow Road, City suffered a surprise 3-1 defeat at Preston North End - one of only two away defeats all season.

MARIO VRANCIC NETS THE FIRST AT ELLAND ROAD

Farke's men responded perfectly to their Deepdale disappointment with an eight-match winning run that took them to the brink of promotion. A run of four draws at the business end of the season was followed by memorable wins over Blackburn Rovers and Aston Villa as City secured both Premier League promotion and then the Championship title.

HERNANDEZ CELEBRATES
WITH MAX AARONS AFTER
HIS OPENER V IPSWICH

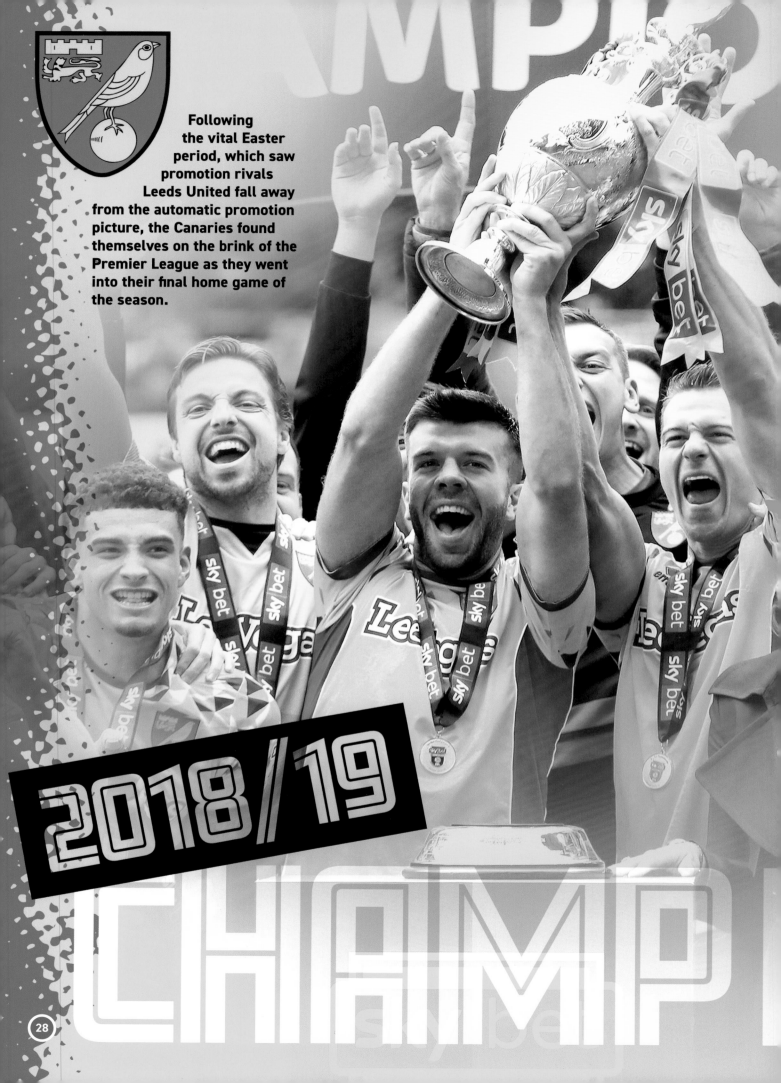

Following the vital Easter period, which saw promotion rivals Leeds United fall away from the automatic promotion picture, the Canaries found themselves on the brink of the Premier League as they went into their final home game of the season.

2018/19

CHAMP

Daniel Farke's men knew that just a point would secure them a place back among the big guns of English football. In all of Norwich City previous nine post-war promotions, only once had the team secured promotion at Carrow Road and that was back in the 1959/60 season as City stepped up from the Third to Second Division.

With Blackburn Rovers the visitors and the Sky television cameras in situ at Carrow Road, the atmosphere was rocking and the scene set for a Saturday evening special. The Canaries did not disappoint.

Marco Stiepermann struck from all of 20 yards to give Norwich a 13th-minute lead and get the game off to the best possible of starts.

Eight minutes later and Norwich were in dreamland as Mario Vrancic crashed home a sublime effort from 25 yards out to double City's lead. Despite Blackburn's Lewis Travis reducing the arrears, City held on for victory and the final whistle was met with wild celebrations as the Carrow Road crowd saluted their promotion-winning heroes.

With promotion achieved, City headed off to Villa Park on the final day of the season with the aim of securing the Championship title. Farke's men had a three-point cushion, but an inferior goal difference to second-placed Sheffield United, so knew they had to avoid defeat against Play-Off bound Aston Villa to guarantee top spot. Goals from Teemu Pukki and Mario Vrancic secured victory as City were confirmed champions by a five-point margin after the Blades could only draw their final fixture at Stoke City.

MARIO VRANCIC SCORES AT VILLA

The Canaries were then presented with the famous Football League trophy in front of their mass of travelling fans on an unforgettable afternoon in the Midlands.

MARCO STIEPERMANN V ROVERS

IONS

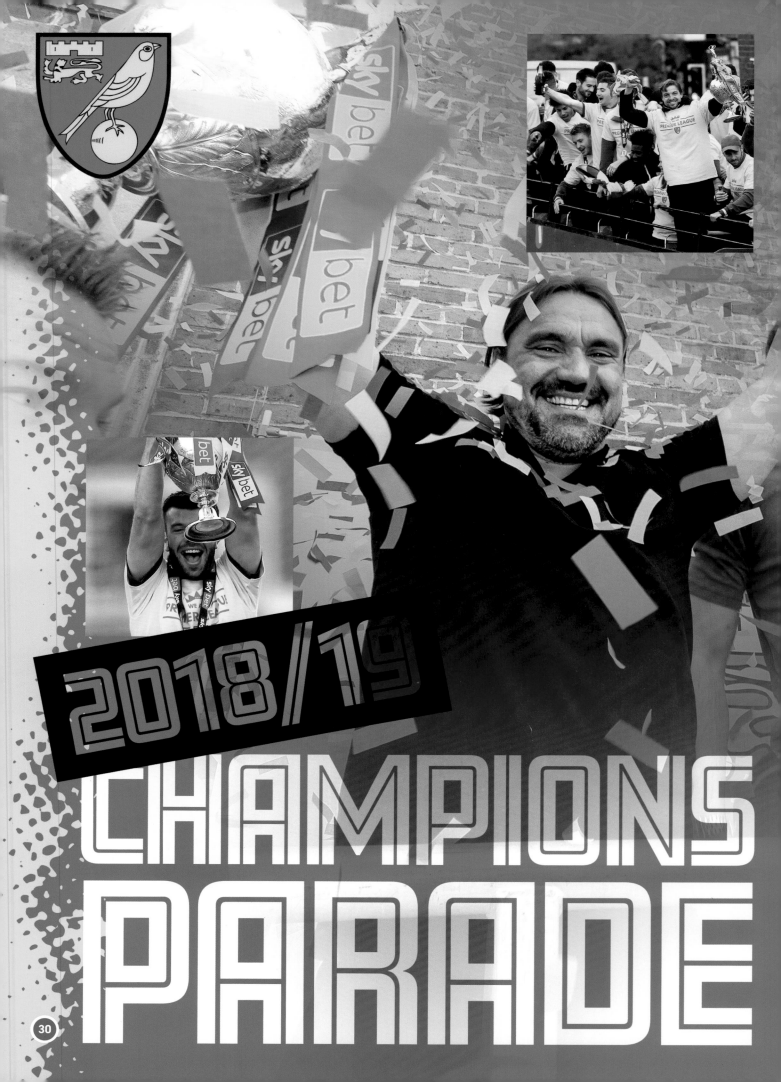

2018/19
CHAMPIONS
PARADE

Following the title triumph at Villa Park, the City squad and management took part in the traditional civic reception at Norwich City Hall and an open-top bus ride around the city the following day.

Tens of thousands of delighted Canary fans lined the route to applaud their current heroes before heading down to Carrow Road to watch two former Canaries, Russell Martin and Wes Hoolahan, plus a host of former club greats take part in a charity match to mark Martin's and Hoolahan's loyal and lengthy Canary careers.

THE LEGEND
BRYAN GUNN

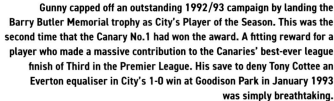

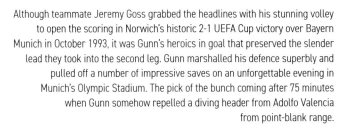

After joining the Canaries in October 1986, Bryan Gunn recorded his first clean sheet in his third game at the club. Gunn and his new teammates kept Manchester United at bay in a goalless draw at Carrow Road on 15 November 1986. The clean sheet was particularly satisfying for Gunn as it came against a side managed by Alex Ferguson, who was Gunn's former boss at Aberdeen and the man that sanctioned his move to Norfolk. Ironically, the point earned by United at Carrow Road was the first point the Red Devils won under the management of Ferguson.

Gunny capped off an outstanding 1992/93 campaign by landing the Barry Butler Memorial trophy as City's Player of the Season. This was the second time that the Canary No.1 had won the award. A fitting reward for a player who made a massive contribution to the Canaries' best-ever league finish of Third in the Premier League. His save to deny Tony Cottee an Everton equaliser in City's 1-0 win at Goodison Park in January 1993 was simply breathtaking.

Although teammate Jeremy Goss grabbed the headlines with his stunning volley to open the scoring in Norwich's historic 2-1 UEFA Cup victory over Bayern Munich in October 1993, it was Gunn's heroics in goal that preserved the slender lead they took into the second leg. Gunn marshalled his defence superbly and pulled off a number of impressive saves on an unforgettable evening in Munich's Olympic Stadium. The pick of the bunch coming after 75 minutes when Gunn somehow repelled a diving header from Adolfo Valencia from point-blank range.

Gunn always enjoyed playing against Liverpool at Anfield and recorded an impressive hat-trick of consecutive clean sheets against the Reds in the late 1980s. However, one of his most impressive Anfield displays came on 30 April 1994 when Norwich faced Liverpool in the Reds' final home game of the season and the club's last-ever match in front of the famous Kop terrace. Once again, Gunn rose to the Anfield challenge and became the last goalkeeper to record a clean sheet in front of the Kop as Norwich won the match 1-0 thanks to a Jeremy Goss goal at the Kop end.

In the final month of Gunn's Norwich City playing career, the Carrow Road favourite produced a memorable performance as City defeated promotion-chasing Nottingham Forest 1-0 at Carrow Road in January 1998. Iwan Roberts netted the game's only goal early in the second-half, but is was Gunn heroics in the City goal that the game was always remembered for - particularly a flying save to claw away a free-kick from Pierre van Hooijdonk that appeared destined for the top corner of the River End goal.

Colour in this picture of Canaries star Jamal Lewis

12

JAMAL
LEWIS

35

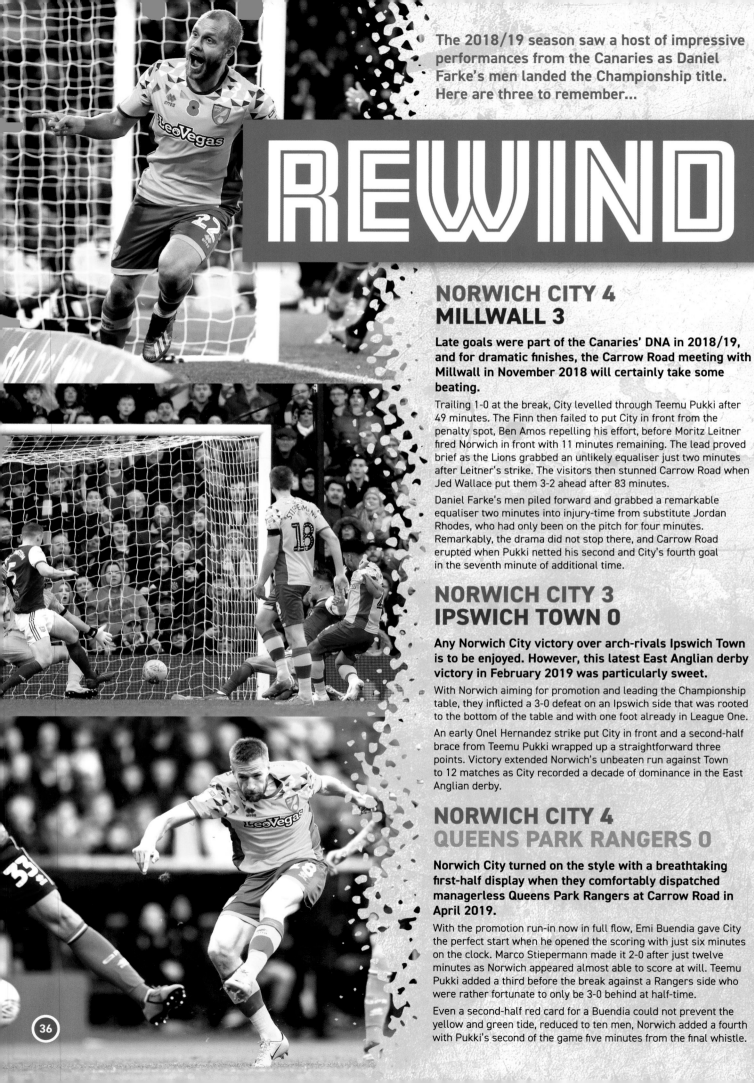

The 2018/19 season saw a host of impressive performances from the Canaries as Daniel Farke's men landed the Championship title. Here are three to remember...

REWIND

NORWICH CITY 4
MILLWALL 3

Late goals were part of the Canaries' DNA in 2018/19, and for dramatic finishes, the Carrow Road meeting with Millwall in November 2018 will certainly take some beating.

Trailing 1-0 at the break, City levelled through Teemu Pukki after 49 minutes. The Finn then failed to put City in front from the penalty spot, Ben Amos repelling his effort, before Moritz Leitner fired Norwich in front with 11 minutes remaining. The lead proved brief as the Lions grabbed an unlikely equaliser just two minutes after Leitner's strike. The visitors then stunned Carrow Road when Jed Wallace put them 3-2 ahead after 83 minutes.

Daniel Farke's men piled forward and grabbed a remarkable equaliser two minutes into injury-time from substitute Jordan Rhodes, who had only been on the pitch for four minutes. Remarkably, the drama did not stop there, and Carrow Road erupted when Pukki netted his second and City's fourth goal in the seventh minute of additional time.

NORWICH CITY 3
IPSWICH TOWN 0

Any Norwich City victory over arch-rivals Ipswich Town is to be enjoyed. However, this latest East Anglian derby victory in February 2019 was particularly sweet.

With Norwich aiming for promotion and leading the Championship table, they inflicted a 3-0 defeat on an Ipswich side that was rooted to the bottom of the table and with one foot already in League One.

An early Onel Hernandez strike put City in front and a second-half brace from Teemu Pukki wrapped up a straightforward three points. Victory extended Norwich's unbeaten run against Town to 12 matches as City recorded a decade of dominance in the East Anglian derby.

NORWICH CITY 4
QUEENS PARK RANGERS 0

Norwich City turned on the style with a breathtaking first-half display when they comfortably dispatched managerless Queens Park Rangers at Carrow Road in April 2019.

With the promotion run-in now in full flow, Emi Buendia gave City the perfect start when he opened the scoring with just six minutes on the clock. Marco Stiepermann made it 2-0 after just twelve minutes as Norwich appeared almost able to score at will. Teemu Pukki added a third before the break against a Rangers side who were rather fortunate to only be 3-0 behind at half-time.

Even a second-half red card for a Buendia could not prevent the yellow and green tide, reduced to ten men, Norwich added a fourth with Pukki's second of the game five minutes from the final whistle.

Answer these questions on the 2018/19 campaign and see how much attention you were paying LAST SEASON!

1. Who made the most League appearances for the Canaries last season?

ANSWER

2. Who netted Norwich City's first Championship goal last season?

ANSWER

3. How many points did the Canaries finish the 2018/19 season with?

ANSWER

4. How many League goals did Norwich City score last season?

ANSWER

5. What was the highest home attendance of 2018/19?

ANSWER

6. Against which three clubs did Norwich City hit four league goals?

ANSWER

7. Who scored a hat-trick in the EFL Cup win at Wycombe Wanderers?

ANSWER

8. Who knocked City out of the FA Cup in the third round?

ANSWER

9. Who received the most yellow cards in the league last season?

ANSWER

10. Who was the only player to receive a red card in the league during 2018/19?

ANSWER

11. Who did the Canaries sign from Brighton & Hove Albion in July 2018?

ANSWER

12. Who top-scored for Norwich City in the league last season?

ANSWER

ANSWERS ON PAGE 62

FAST FORWARD

There are lots of exciting games ahead for the Canaries in the second half of the 2019/20 Premier League campaign.

Here are three potential crackers...

TOTTENHAM HOTSPUR (A)
22 JANUARY 2020

A first visit to the new Tottenham Hotspur Stadium on Wednesday 22 January 2020 is one of City's standout Premier League fixtures.

The combination of playing at Spurs' breathtaking new home and facing a side that reached the 2019 Champions League Final really makes this one of City's most eagerly awaited games of the season.

No doubt this will be a tough challenge on the pitch for Daniel's Farke's men against one of the Premier League strongest sides. However, the City fans will take confidence in knowing their heroes have defeated Spurs away in the Premier League as recently as 2012 when Elliott Bennett struck a memorable second-half winner in a 2-1 triumph.

LIVERPOOL (H)
8 FEBRUARY 2020

Norwich City will welcome 2019 Champions League winners Liverpool to Carrow Road on 8 February 2020 as German coaches Daniel Farke and Jurgen Klopp go head-to-head.

The Reds' last visit to Norfolk resulted in a Premier League classic as Liverpool edged a nine-goal thriller 5-4. Sebastien Bassong appeared to have rescued a point for City in the 90th minute only for Adam Lallana to net a last-gasp injury-time winner for Liverpool.

Having ended last season as Premier League runners-up, the Anfield club will be keen to go one better in 2019/20 and this will therefore be another massive test for the Canaries, but one they will no doubt be relishing.

MANCHESTER CITY (A)
17 MAY 2020

Manchester City landed a clean sweep of the domestic honours in 2018/19 and will be aiming for a third consecutive Premier League title in 2019/20.

A final-day fixture at the Etihad Stadium is about as tough as it gets. However, competing in the Premier League is all about pitting your wits against the best and they certainly don't come any better than Pep Guardiola's men.

So although the Canaries' season concludes with a mammoth task against the champions, it is a challenge Norwich have risen to before. They visited the Etihad on the final day of the 2012/13 Premier League season when goals from Anthony Pilkington, Grant Holt and a wonderful solo effort from Jonny Howson secured Norwich a 3-2 victory.

PREMIER LEAGUE

OUR PREDICTION FOR PREMIER LEAGUE WINNERS:

LIVERPOOL

YOUR PREDICTION:

OUR PREDICTION FOR PREMIER LEAGUE RUNNERS-UP:

MANCHESTER CITY

YOUR PREDICTION:

CHAMPIONSHIP

OUR PREDICTION FOR CHAMPIONSHIP WINNERS:

LEEDS UNITED

YOUR PREDICTION:

OUR PREDICTION FOR CHAMPIONSHIP RUNNERS-UP:

DERBY COUNTY

YOUR PREDICTION:

THE FA CUP

OUR PREDICTION FOR FA CUP WINNERS:

NORWICH CITY

YOUR PREDICTION:

OUR PREDICTION FOR FA CUP RUNNERS-UP:

MANCHESTER UNITED

YOUR PREDICTION:

EFL CUP

OUR PREDICTION FOR EFL CUP WINNERS:

LEICESTER CITY

YOUR PREDICTION:

OUR PREDICTION FOR EFL CUP RUNNERS-UP:

WEST HAM UNITED

YOUR PREDICTION:

2020 PREDICTIONS

TEAM WORK

Every Premier League team is hidden in the grid, except one!

Can you figure out which is missing?

Arsenal

Aston Villa

Bournemouth

Brighton and Hove Albion

Burnley

Chelsea

Crystal Palace

Everton

Leicester City

Liverpool

Manchester City

Manchester United

Newcastle United

Norwich City

Sheffield United

Southampton

Tottenham Hotspur

Watford

West Ham United

Wolverhampton Wanderers

J T S E W A K B M R R A T S T C B
E S O T E A S T O N V I L L A R Y
A Q E T S N N B H T E U F T E Y S
E B A O T A P R U V P B K Q O S D
V O J D H E S I M R D B I E V T N
I U T C A W N G E B N U C H I A Z
F R X E M R L H E Y F L K J M L P
M N J G U S I T A I Y O E A E P U
A E H O N R U O N M H X G Y P A S
O M B N I E S N F J H L N W L L A
Y O D K T R Z A N J M O D Q R A P
T U E Z E E H N O H R E T A E C Y
I T T Y D D S D R K L E S S A E T
C H I U F N J H W I S B L S P C I
R N N D A A S O I W U E F P B U C
E F U H G W H V C A H M X D V B R
T E E I F N T E H C N F C G L Y E
S P L R F O E A C D C J I E T V T
E Y T N S T G L I V E R P O O L S
C W S O S P E B T R P G N Y F K E
I W A I V M D I Y V R I B E V H H
E Z C N D A K O E H X E M V I O C
L Q W E L H R N G O M O A E C H N
S M E J K R J S E W R N R R K U A
M A N C H E S T E R U N I T E D M
J A H G U V X B N N I G G O U T H
D I X A F L W M M Y A C L N V H C
C S D O J O L E K Y Z L T B Q S X
K Q B N T W A T F O R D W S Z I P
L F B Y U H N O T P M A H T U O S

ANSWERS ON PAGE 62

TODD CANTWELL

Q Ex-Hammer who made his debut for the Golden Boys last season

Middlesbrough keeper who played all 46 league games last season **R**

Joint Premier League top scorer last season alongside teammate Mané and Arsenal's Aubameyang

S

N France international who joined Spurs from Olympique Lyonnais in July 2019

O Goalkeeper and local lad who came through the ranks at Norwich

Nickname of Yorkshire club Barnsley **T**

U The Clarets' team kit manufacturer

P Former England international in the manager's seat at Craven Cottage

The home of Championship new boys Charlton Athletic **V**

42

W
Managed the Blades to promotion to the Premier League

X
Switzerland international who plays his home games at the Emirates Stadium

2019/20   PART 2

WHO'S WHO & WHAT'S WHAT OF ENGLISH FOOTBALL?

Y
The Magpies' international right-back with over 50 USA caps

Z
Hammers defender capped over 50 times by Argentina

ANSWERS ON PAGE 62

BURNLEY
TURF MOOR
CAPACITY: 22,546

MANCHESTER CITY
ETIHAD STADIUM
CAPACITY: 55,097

MANCHESTER UTD
OLD TRAFFORD
CAPACITY: 76,000

EVERTON
GOODISON PARK
CAPACITY: 39,572

LIVERPOOL
ANFIELD
CAPACITY: 54,074

LEICESTER CITY
KING POWER STADIUM
CAPACITY: 32,312

WOLVES
MOLINEUX STADIUM
CAPACITY: 31,700

ASTON VILLA
VILLA PARK
CAPACITY: 42,785

WATFORD
VICARAGE ROAD
CAPACITY: 21,577

SOUTHAMPTON
ST MARY'S STADIUM
CAPACITY: 32,384

BOURNEMOUTH
VITALITY STADIUM
CAPACITY: 11,329

NEWCASTLE UTD
ST JAMES' PARK
CAPACITY: 52,405

PREMIER LEAGUE GROUNDS 2019/20

Take a look at where the Canaries will be heading this season to take on their rivals.

Tick the grounds off once we've visited!

SHEFFIELD UTD
BRAMALL LANE
CAPACITY: 32,702

NORWICH CITY
CARROW ROAD
CAPACITY: 27,244

ARSENAL
EMIRATES STADIUM
CAPACITY: 60,260

TOTTENHAM HOTSPUR
TOTTENHAM HOTSPUR STADIUM
CAPACITY: 62,062

WEST HAM UTD
LONDON STADIUM
CAPACITY: 66,000

CRYSTAL PALACE
SELHURST PARK
CAPACITY: 25,456

CHELSEA
STAMFORD BRIDGE
CAPACITY: 41,631

BRIGHTON & HA
AMERICAN EXPRESS
COMMUNITY STADIUM
CAPACITY: 30,666

FAN"

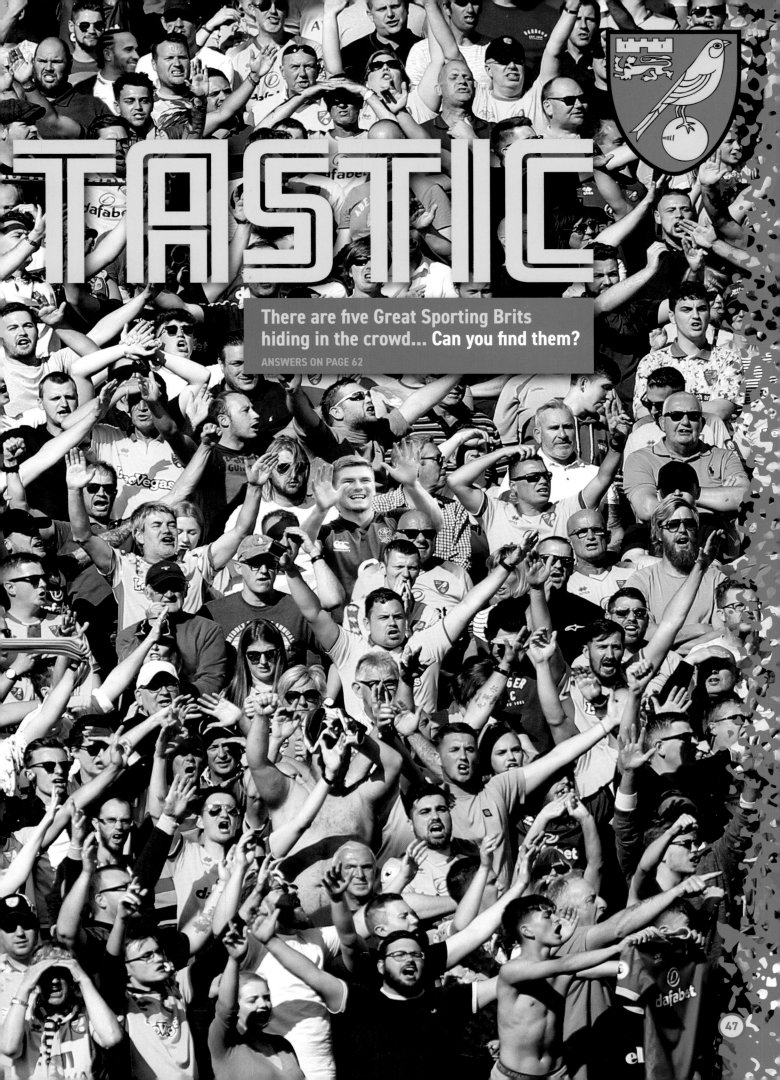

TASTIC

There are five Great Sporting Brits hiding in the crowd... Can you find them?

ANSWERS ON PAGE 62

47

ANSWERS ON PAGE 62

THE LEGEND
DEAN ASHTON

Striker Dean Ashton marked his Carrow Road debut with a goal against Middlesbrough on 22 January 2005. All eyes were on Ashton following his £3M record move from Crewe Alexandra. Despite taking an 18th-minute lead, Norwich found themselves trailing 4-1 when Ashton popped up with this first Premier League goal ten minutes from time. His debut strike sparked an incredible finale as City levelled the game with two goals in the last two minutes.

Ashton's third goal for the Canaries helped Nigel Worthington's side to their standout result of the 2004/05 campaign, after he opened the scoring in a 2-0 victory over Manchester United at Carrow Road on 9 April 2005. Ashton met a beautifully weighted free-kick from David Bentley ten minutes into the second half and guided a firm header past Tim Howard from the edge of the area at the River End to spark scenes of delight at Carrow Road. Leon McKenzie added a second 11 minutes later in a memorable 2-0 victory.

Dean Ashton was the Canaries' two-goal hero in a pulsating Premier League match against relegation rivals Crystal Palace in the latter stages of the 2004/05 season. With Palace also rumoured to have been chasing his signature when he opted to join the Canaries, this impressive showing against the Eagles showed the Selhurst Park crowed just what they were missing. Ashton's first goal of the afternoon came after 22 minutes to level the match at 1-1 and the ace marksman then fired City in front right at the start of the season-half. An eventful clash ended 3-3.

With Norwich City battling for their Premier League status in April 2005, Ashton was once again the toast of Carrow Road, heading home a crucial late winner to seal a 2-1 triumph. A wonder-strike from Youssef Safri gave Norwich a 1-0 lead midway through the second-half. The Moroccan's goal looked as though it would secure all three points until Patrick Kluivert levelled in the 89th minute. However, Ashton turned despair into delirium, heading home his fourth goal in three games to grab all three precious points.

Following the Canaries' final day relegation from the Premier League in May 2005, Dean Ashton became a wanted man by a number of Premier League clubs. City's prized asset continued to plunder goals in the 2005/06 Championship campaign. In December 2005, he scored his final goals at Carrow Road to give Norwich all three points when he netted a hat-trick in 3-1 victory over Southampton. The City man sent two headers and a stunning volley past Saints' keeper Antti Niemi in a man-of-the-match performance.

PREMIER
LEAGUE 2019/20

ARSENAL

ASTON VILLA

BOURNEMOUTH

BRIGHTON & HA

BURNLEY

CHELSEA

CRYSTAL PALACE

EVERTON

LEICESTER CITY

In a yellow & green world, get to know your rivals in full Premier League colour!

LIVERPOOL

MANCHESTER CITY

MANCHESTER UNITED

NEWCASTLE UNITED

NORWICH CITY

SHEFFIELD UNITED

SOUTHAMPTON

TOTTENHAM HOTSPUR

WATFORD

WEST HAM UNITED

WOLVES

TEEMU
PUKKI

2018/19
PLAYER
OF THE
SEASON

ACADEMY PLAYER OF THE SEASON

Star striker Teemu Pukki capped of a memorable debut campaign with the Canaries by collecting the Barry Butler Memorial Trophy as City's 2018/19 Player of the Season.

Pukki edged out Christoph Zimmermann and Emi Buendia, who came second and third respectively in the end-of-season supporters' poll.

The 29-year-old was handed the prestigious Barry Butler Memorial Trophy by joint majority shareholder's Delia Smith and Michael Wynn Jones ahead of City's promotion-winning final home game of the season against Blackburn Rovers.

He followed in the footsteps of a host of City heroes such as Martin Peters, Bryan Gunn, Robert Fleck, Iwan Roberts, Grant Holt, Wes Hoolahan, and James Maddison who won the award in 2017/18.

The Finnish international joined City on a free transfer from Brondby ahead of the 2018/19 season and immediately hit the ground running, scoring in his opening outing at Carrow Road in August against West Bromwich Albion.

The ace marksman went on to score 30 goals in all competitions with 29 of them in the league, making him the top scorer in the Sky Bet Championship.

Pukki's 29-goal haul in the Championship played a vital part in the Canaries' 2018/19 title-winning success. His last-gasp winners against Millwall and Bolton, plus a brace in the 3-0 victory over Ipswich Town provided some truly memorable moments in an unforgettable campaign.

As well as being voted the Canaries' Player of the Season, Pukki was also named in the PFA and Sky Bet Championship teams of the season, as well as winning the Sky Bet Championship Player of the Season award at the Football League Awards.

ADAM IDAH

While Teemu Pukki landed the Barry Butler Memorial Trophy as the Canaries' 2018/19 Player of the Season, fellow striker Adam Idah was presented with the Etty Smith award as the Academy Player of the Season.

The pacy frontman netted 13 goals from 24 appearances for the Academy under-23 side and his form was rewarded with international recognition with the Republic of Ireland at under-21 level.

The 18-year-old has since been elevated to training with the first-team squad and travelled to Germany for the Canaries' pre-season tour.

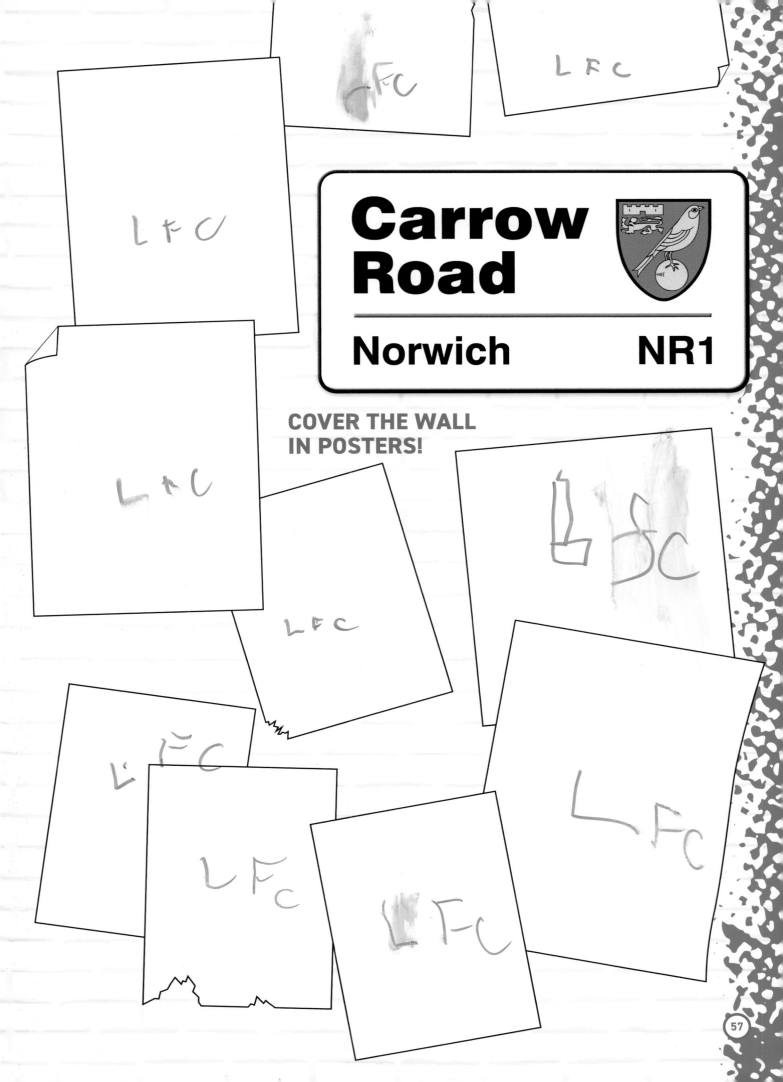

Carrow Road

Norwich NR1

COVER THE WALL IN POSTERS!

Norwich City have boasted a wealth of talent over the years!

Here is our...

CANARIES DREAM TEAM

...see if you agree!

GOALKEEPER

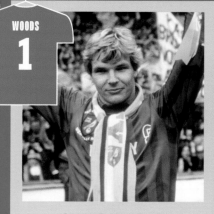

WOODS
1

CHRIS WOODS

Ultra-reliable goalkeeper Chris Woods was a Wembley winner with City in the 1985 League Cup Final. Blessed with lightning reflexes, Woods had an ability to make the most difficult of saves with the minimum of fuss. He won full international recognition with England while at Carrow Road.

YOUR CHOICE

DEFENDER

CULVERHOUSE
2

IAN CULVERHOUSE

A consistent performer for the Canaries throughout the late '80s and early '90s, Ian Culverhouse amassed 369 appearances for the club. He was a vital member of the 1992/93 side that finished third in the Premier League and then competed in the UEFA Cup.

YOUR CHOICE

MIDFIELDER

PETERS
6

MARTIN PETERS

A World Cup-winner with England in 1966, Martin Peters arrived at Carrow Road in 1975 and helped inspire promotion to the top flight. A star performer as City established themselves in the First Division, Peters was the Canaries' star man as John Bond's side thrilled Carrow Road with an impressive brand of free-flowing passing football.

YOUR CHOICE

MIDFIELDER

FOX
7

RUEL FOX

Winger Ruel Fox progressed through the youth and reserve ranks at Norwich City, before going on to thrill the Carrow Road crowd with his tricky skills and blistering pace. An integral part of Mike Walker's successful teams in 1992/93 and 1993/94, Fox had the ability to terrorise opposition full-backs.

YOUR CHOICE

MIDFIELDER

TOWNSEND
8

ANDY TOWNSEND

A true box-to-box midfield dynamo, Andy Townsend formed an excellent midfield partnership with Ian Crook in 1988/89 as City went in pursuit of a league and cup double. His Carrow Road form was rewarded with a call-up to the Republic of Ireland squad and a big-money move to Chelsea.

YOUR CHOICE

DEFENDER

BOWEN
3

MARK BOWEN

Attacking full-back Mark Bowen was a polished performer at Carrow Road and had the great ability to make overlapping runs and pop up with goals. It was Bowen who netted City's winning goal away to Bayern Munich in the 1993/94 UEFA Cup. Very rarely beaten in one-on-one situations, Bowen make 399 appearances for City.

YOUR CHOICE

DEFENDER

WATSON
4

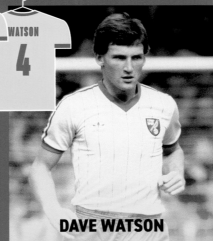

DAVE WATSON

Plucked from Liverpool reserves, Dave Watson proved to be one of many shrewd signings by manager Ken Brown. Watson skippered the Canaries to League Cup glory at Wembley in 1985 and promotion as Second Division champions the following season. He was also capped by England while playing for City.

YOUR CHOICE

DEFENDER

STRINGER
5

DAVE STRINGER

Norfolk-born Dave Stringer was one of Norwich City's finest servants. A key member of the club's 1971/72 team that won the Second Division title and brought First Division football to Norfolk for the first time, Stringer excelled in the top flight and featured in both of City's League Cup finals in the 1970s.

YOUR CHOICE

FORWARD

SUTTON
9

CHRIS SUTTON

Striker Chris Sutton netted an incredible 25 Premier League goals during the 1993/94 season and also led the Canary attack in the successful UEFA Cup campaign. An outstanding target-man, Sutton left Carrow Road for a then record club fee of £5M in July 1994 when he joined Blackburn Rovers.

FORWARD

FLECK
10

ROBERT FLECK

A real crowd pleaser, Robert Fleck had two spells with the Canaries after joining the club initially from Glasgow Rangers in December 1987. Fleck became recognised as one of the First Division's most feared strikers during his first stint at Carrow Road. A scorer of many spectacular goals during his Canary career, Fleck netted 84 times for Norwich City.

YOUR CHOICE

FORWARD

HUCKERBY
11

DARREN HUCKERBY

Unquestionably the most exciting individual to represent the club in the modern era, Darren Huckerby produced countless match-winning performances during the 2004/05 First Division title winning season. The jet-heeled frontman was then voted Player of the Season in the Canaries' 2004/05 Premier League campaign.

YOUR CHOICE

TOP 10

MY TOP 10...

MOMENTS OF THIS YEAR

1.
2.
3.
4.
5.
6.
7.
8.
9.
10.

MY TOP 10...

FOOTBALLERS OF ALL TIME

1.
2.
3.
4.
5.
6.
7.
8.
9.
10.

MY TOP 10...

NORWICH CITY MEMORIES

1.
2.
3.
4.
5.
6.
7.
8.
9.
10.

MY TOP 10...

RESOLUTIONS FOR 2020

1.
2.
3.
4.
5.
6.
7.
8.
9.
10.

60

CAVAN COUNTY LIBRARY

61

QUIZ ANSWERS

PAGE 24 · A-Z PART ONE

A. César Azpilicueta. B. Bristol City.
C. Matty Cash. D. Harlee Dean.
E. The Eagles. F. Thomas Frank, Brentford.
G. Goodison Park. H. Neil Harris.
I. Kelechi Iheanacho. J. Gabriel Jesus.
K. Mateusz Klich. L. Jesse Lingard.
M. Glenn Murray.

PAGE 37 · REWIND

1. Tim Krul, 46.
2. Onel Hernandez v Birmingham City.
3. 94. 4. 93. 5. 27,040 v Ipswich Town.
6. Sheffield Wednesday, Bolton Wanderers and QPR.
7. Jordan Rhodes. 8. Portsmouth.
9. Christoph Zimmermann, 11.
10. Onel Hernández v QPR.
11. Tim Krul. 12. Teemu Pukki 29.

PAGE 40 · TEAM WORK

Sheffield United.

PAGE 42 · A-Z PART TWO

N. Tanguy Ndombele. O. Aston Oxborough.
P. Scott Parker. Q. Domingos Quina.
R. Darren Randolph. S. Mo Salah.
T. The Tykes. U. Umbro. V. The Valley.
W. Chris Wilder. X. Granit Xhaka.
Y. DeAndre Yedlin. Z. Pablo Zabaleta.

PAGE 46 · FAN'TASTIC

Owen Farrell, Lewis Hamilton Johanna Konta,
Anthony Joshua and Ben Stokes.

PAGE 48 · HEY REF!

1. Direct free kick. 2. Indirect free kick.
3. Yellow card - Caution. 4. Red card - Sending off.
5. Obstruction. 6. Substitution. 7. Offside/foul.
8. Penalty. 9. Offside location. 10. Play on.